I0802101

IMAGES
*of America*

# St. Mark United Methodist Church

**On the Cover:** Rev. Matthew Clair Jr. is pictured in 1944 in an unusual pose as he sits front and center among the New Horizon church workers, a group made up of all facets of St. Mark's congregation. (Courtesy of the St. Mark United Methodist Church library.)

IMAGES
*of America*

# St. Mark United Methodist Church

Daniel T. Parker
Foreword by Rev. P. Devon Brown

ARCADIA
PUBLISHING

ISBN 978-1-4671-0328-2

Published by Arcadia Publishing
Charleston, South Carolina

Printed in the United States of America

Library of Congress Control Number: 2018962854

For all general information, please contact Arcadia Publishing:
Telephone 843-853-2070
Fax 843-853-0044
E-mail sales@arcadiapublishing.com
For customer service and orders:
Toll-Free 1-888-313-2665

Visit us on the Internet at www.arcadiapublishing.com

*We dedicate this book to all of those loyal members who have extended their gifts and talents to us, nurtured us, and prayed for St. Mark for the past 125 years, from 1893 to 2018.*

# Contents


Foreword 6

Acknowledgments 7

Introduction 8

1. In the Beginning: The Road We've Trod, 1893–1934 11
2. Building the Future: Upon this Rock I Will Build My Church, 1935–1958 17
3. New Horizons: For Everything There is a Season, 1959–1999 35
4. Looking to the Future: Your Old Shall Dream Dreams; Your Young Shall See Visions, 2000–2018 69

Bibliography 95

# Foreword

In the beginning, God created the heavens and the earth. From that point forward, history has been painting a picture of the Lord's salvific plan in action. In the year 1893, God added another brushstroke to that portrait in the form of St. Mark Methodist Episcopal Church. Since its inception 126 years ago, the ministry of this great congregation has added depth and detail to God's artwork. That detail has been greatly enhanced by the loving relationships of members both past and present. I am personally grateful for the opportunity to be part of the St. Mark brushstroke. From the birth of our first son when I was an associate pastor in the early 1990s, to the launching of our second and final child during this stint as senior pastor, the love of St. Mark members has left an undeniable and indelible imprint on the hearts of Sharon and me.

This book offers a glimpse of that love in action. It is a record of how St. Mark has been used by God to bring the gospel to life. My prayer is that those who read the words contained herein will not only see a brushstroke but will also perceive the larger portrait of salvation available to those who dare believe that Jesus was raised from the grave.

Yours in Christ,
Rev. P. Devon Brown
Senior Pastor, St. Mark United Methodist Church

# ACKNOWLEDGMENTS

Our gratitude is extended to the many parishioners who shared their valuable photographs, books, and manuscripts to enhance the telling of our story. A special thank-you goes to Charles and Beverly Redmond for sharing their historic *Saint Mark's Blue Book*, which offered invaluable information, and to Licia Knight and Lorri Baldwin for the loan of their papers. We are most appreciative of St. Mark's library, which yielded vast information. Deep gratitude goes out to Lynne Lee for the invaluable images shared. A special thank-you goes to the incredible and dedicated 125th Anniversary History Committee, without whose help, support, time, and sharing of knowledge, the completion of this book would not have been possible.

Unless otherwise noted, all images are courtesy of the St. Mark United Methodist Church library.

# INTRODUCTION

The year 1893 was a time for many Chicagoans to celebrate. The long-anticipated World's Columbian Exposition was held on the grounds of Jackson Park and the Midway Plaisance. The Museum of Science and Industry was erected for this occasion on the South Side of Chicago. African Americans were excluded from attendance and participation. The great black female journalist Ida B. Wells, an early leader in the civil rights movement, was angered by this display of racism. She led anti-lynching crusades during the 1890s, and heralded her outrage of African American exclusion from the fair in the mainly African American Chicago newspapers. Meanwhile, only a few blocks away, there occurred a glorious celebration—the founding of St. Mark Methodist Episcopal Church.

It has been 126 years since the founders, Mr. and Mrs. John A. Washington, Mr. and Mrs. Henry Bomar, Mr. and Mrs. Richard Jones, and George T. Jackson gathered in a living room where many meetings would be held. A State Street storefront on Chicago's South Side served as the first home of the historic St. Mark United Methodist Church. In 1893, the church was in the Lexington Conference and named St. Mark Methodist Episcopal Church. The founders were God-fearing individuals who were proud, humble, and gifted people seeking higher ground. They established, with the guidance of Bishop W.F. Andrews, district superintendent G.R. Bryant, pastor H.N. Carol, and pastor S.C. Gooseley, a heterogeneous congregation with similar characters of spirit and aspiration. Many had migrated to Chicago from the South in search of better opportunities for themselves and their families.

Many of the parishioners had escaped the harshness and atrocities of the South only 30 years previously. Engulfed in the throngs of the Great Depression, they knew their faith would allow them to survive. Many others were born in Chicago and resided in the vicinity of Fiftieth Street and Wabash Avenue. Most parishioners attended Wendell Phillips High School, built in 1904, which sits on the corner of East Pershing Road and South Prairie Avenue. In 1935, they embraced the newly built Jean Baptiste Point DuSable High School, erected at Forty-Ninth Street and Wabash Avenue across the street from the church. DuSable was the first high school in Chicago built exclusively for African Americans. The school was named after the first permanent, non–Native American settler in Chicago, a black pioneer who was born in Haiti of Haitian and African descent. This ambitious trapper developed a prosperous trading post and farm on the north bank of the Chicago River around the 1780s. Jean Baptiste Point Du Sable is known as the Father of Chicago, as St. Mark became known as the mother church for black Methodism in Chicago.

With such a strong legacy, these determined people of faith were on the path that God had set before them, and they knew with his hand upon them they would not fail. Hebrews 11:6 reads, "But without faith it is impossible to please Him, for he who comes to God must believe that He is, and that He is a rewarder of those who diligently seek Him." The founders of the church would need that faith for the troubled years that lay ahead.

With World War I a not so distant memory, and with the Second World War in full force, these people of God forged ahead. The church was proud to produce the only black United Service Organizations (USO) during World War II. During the war, membership grew to 3,000, and by the grace of God, the church experienced no wartime casualties.

From its inception and throughout its long history, the members of St. Mark established numerous organizations. One of the founders of St. Mark, Nellie Bomar, led the first gospel choir. Later, in 1933, Walter Gossette was appointed director of the senior choir and remained as minister of music for 30 years. In 1900, the Woman's Home Missionary Society was formed, and in 1905, the Ladies' Aid Society. The Methodist Brotherhood Service was formed in 1915, the Willing Workers was formed in 1917, and the Women's Master's Queenly Reserves was established in 1924. In 1935, the first black Cub Scout pack was formed, St. Mark Cub Pack 3534, with Floy Burdette as den mother and Leonard O. Lee as scoutmaster. In 1948, the troop included a young man named Robert Sublette, who later became a scoutmaster. And there was a young man named Ronald Temple who joined the pack; he later became chancellor of the City Colleges of Chicago. In 1938, Dorothy Porter Welles organized the local Girl Scouts, and went on to do many astonishing things with the troop. In 1961, Emma Thomas became a Girl Scout leader whose tenure spanned over three decades. Combined with the leadership of Narcissa Roberts (Daisy Troop), Lu Alice Ray (Brownie Troop), and Meryl Shands (Junior Troop), St. Mark girls learned various skills, earned patches and merit badges, and experienced camping. They had the pleasure of visiting the home of Juliette Gordon Low, founder of the Girl Scouts. This group of Scouts was known for selling more cookies than any other troop in the Chicago metropolitan area.

Today, many of these organizations' names have changed. The Methodist Brotherhood became the United Methodist Men (UMM), and in 1967 the Women's Society of Christian Services became the United Methodist Women (UMW)—to name but two. Yet all of these organizations are still growing and making a difference in the lives of others, both in the church and in the community.

During those early days, many of the top colleges and universities in the United States were populated with students from St. Mark United Methodist Church. These stellar students performed at the top of their class. The astonishing congregation then was made up of dedicated, highly skilled domestics, doctors, teachers, high-ranking government officials, and people from every walk of life. In the corporate world, there was Henry Rivers, a St. Mark member and the first black manager at a nationwide grocery store chain, the Great Atlantic & Pacific Tea Company (A&P). J. Ernest Wilkins Sr., the first African American to serve in a US subcabinet position, in the Eisenhower administration, was also from this congregation. Wilkins had two sons, and one received his doctorate at the age of 18 and developed the only doctoral program at a black university, Howard University, at that time. His brother, also a member of the church, worked on the *Harvard Law Review*. The church also had as a member a female educator who was the superintendent of schools in the second-largest city in the United States at the time. "Son of the church" William Carter became a pastor and then a high-ranking officer of the church; he raised over a billion dollars for the United Methodist Church. The church's countless pastors journeyed on to become bishops and other leaders in the United Methodist denomination. These determined worshipers gave to their church abundantly with their gifts of talent, finances, and themselves. This was the bedrock of St. Mark United Methodist Church—strong people of faith. Every day, she writes her story as she goes about doing the work of God and giving him the praise and the glory, as in Psalms 75:1: "We give thanks to You, O God, we give thanks! For Your wondrous works declare that Your name is near."

# *One*

# In the Beginning

## The Road We've Trod, 1893–1934

*St. Mark has not always occupied a "place in the sun." Step by step and breath by breath we have come over a rugged road—adding here a little, there a little, until here we are! It is a long way from the little store front to 50th [and Wabash Avenue]. We came from the store front: we are on our way to the bigger, better thing.*

—*Saint Mark's Blue Book*, 1933–1934

The year 1893 was pivotal for black Methodists in Chicago because St. Mark Methodist Episcopal church was established. Much work and prayer led to this historic occasion. Interest crystallized in 1892 at the general conference held in Omaha, Nebraska. Here, official action was taken authorizing the Lexington Annual Conference to establish Methodism in Chicago among African Americans. Later, in March 1893, a definitive program for the development of St. Mark was established at the annual session of the Lexington Conference held in Shelbyville, Kentucky. Bishop R.S. Foster was presiding, and Rev. S.C. Goosely was appointed pastor. The following year, 1894, Rev. E.A. White was appointed pastor, but before his tenure ended he was called to Cleveland, Ohio. In 1895, under the leadership of the newly appointed Rev. George E. Curry, St. Mark was formally incorporated. This long anticipated event occurred in the home of John and Flora Washington. Henry and Nellie Bomar, Mr. and Mrs. Richard Moore, Richard Jones, and George Jackson were also instrumental in the church's founding. The first services for St. Mark Methodist Episcopal Church were held in a storefront called Apollo Hall. During 1895, the Chicago Missionary and Church Extension Board paid $25 per month for nine months and then withdrew its assistance. St. Mark moved from Thirty-Third and State Streets to Forty-Seventh and State Streets. This was a church building called Old State Street Methodist Church, which had been vacated by a white congregation because of fire. For two years, the St. Mark congregation worked diligently at restoring the edifice only to have the white congregation reclaim it. As there were no rights of equality for African Americans in 1897, they had little choice but to vacate the premises.

In 1897, St. Mark began worshipping in a storeroom on West Forty-Seventh Street near Dearborn Street. In 1899, Rev. John W. Robinson was appointed pastor, with membership of 25 parishioners. New hope sprang up in the hearts of that small group. The first sermon Robinson preached was on Easter Sunday.

The coming of Reverend Robinson marked a new era in both St. Mark and Chicago for Methodism among African Americans. Under his inspiration, intelligence, and fiscal acumen, St. Mark returned to the State Street property previously owned by a white congregation. The congregation purchased the property for $8,000, with an initial payment of $4,000, in May 1900. In September 1902, the members were able to burn the mortgage. In 1903, the Lexington Conference held its annual session at St. Mark, with Bishop John M. Walden presiding.

With the meeting of the general conference in Chicago, many interested and influential African American Methodist men and women of means, with deep faith and a strong spirit of hope, were drawn to this enlightened congregation. As a result, the church grew steadily in membership and financial responsibility.

After Reverend Robinson left St. Mark, Rev. W.C. Stovall became pastor and served from 1907 to 1910. During his pastorate, St. Mark purchased the building at Fiftieth Street and Wabash Avenue, which would become the grand structure of the day. This church was purchased from the same white congregation that had previously owned the Old State Street Methodist Church. When the membership grew to 2,200, they had outgrown the building. This robust congregation planned to add a main auditorium to the existing structure. But in their effort to construct an addition, St. Mark experienced financial challenges. Reverend Stovall was followed by Rev. H.A. Foreman, who gave St. Mark two successful years of service.

In 1910, the parishioners sold bonds to fund the St. Mark building project. With the return of Rev. J.W. Robinson, the famous "Gold Bond" issue was an enormously successful financial project, which in turn made possible the building of the new auditorium adjoining the Sunday school. Reverend Robinson remained at St. Mark for 11 years. He left for New York to pastor the New York St. Mark Methodist Episcopal Church.

By April 1923, St. Mark had cleared its debt and maintained a thriving membership. By God's grace, St. Mark became a leader in the Lexington Conference, and ready for a new pastor, Rev. J.B. Redmond. Reverend Redmond was appointed the new pastor of St. Mark and moved with his wife, Josephine, from Cleveland to assume the position of senior pastor. Reverend Redmond was no stranger to St. Mark, as he had been a lay member of the church and had served briefly as an assistant pastor. Because of the diligence of its members, St. Mark was able to meet the annual apportionment of $3,000. Under Reverend Redmond's leadership, many new organizations were established and programs enlarged. Organizations such as the Ladies' Aid Society (1905), Woman's Aid of Foreign Service (1911), the Woodlawn Sewing Circle, the Ruth Gleaners, the Invincibles (1928), and St. Mark Scout Cub Pack No. 3534 ("Hey!"), with Floy Burnett as den mother, in 1935.

Many St. Markers, although well established, were sometimes overlooked. They were the glue that held the church together. One was Jannie Hester Vance. She was born in 1860 in Austin, Texas. She moved to Chicago in 1912 and joined her beloved St. Mark in 1916. She was an active member until around 1940, when she moved to Inkster, Michigan. Jannie's sight begin to fail around 1950, and that is when her grandson Patric Mc Coy stepped in. He read her the *Messenger* every week. Jannie remained devoted to St. Mark until her death. She lived to the ripe age of 98.

There was the loyal husband-and-wife team of Melinda Caroline McKissack and Robert Elias Watkins. They left a legacy that lives to the present day. They migrated to Chicago from Nashville, Tennessee, in or about 1912. Melinda had a historical connection to the Methodist Church, having been reared by her brother Alexander McKissack, who was a circuit rider Methodist pastor in Tennessee. In addition, she obtained a college diploma in 1898 from Central Tennessee College, a freedman's college sponsored by the Methodist Church. She received a teaching certification for the primary grades in Davidson County, Tennessee. They were the parents of Earline (John Dailey), Thelma (Walter Gibson) and Robert Watkins (Hannah Bowman). In 1912, they joined St. Mark Methodist Episcopal Church, where Melinda taught Sunday school for nearly 30 years before her passing in 1940. Thelma and Walter Gibson had nine children: Kenneth, Gloria, Walter Jr., Robert W.E., Winona, Carole, Roland, Sharon, and Paula. All attended St. Mark and were active members. The Watkins legacy continues at St. Mark. On August 17, 2009, John Lewis, who was the St. Mark chair of the Committee on Race and Religion Ministry, conducted a Careers in Foreign Service Forum. The descendants of Melinda McKissack and Robert Watkins were the presenters: David Mosby, the political advisor to the US embassy in Dakar, Senegal, and Rebekah Eubanks, legal advisor to the US Agency for International Development.

St. Mark continued to grow, and by the mid-1930s, the congregants had once again outgrown the building. Under Reverend Redmond's leadership, a building campaign was launched. A new lot was purchased at Fiftieth Street and Michigan Avenue for $40,000, with a $25,000 down payment. The new St. Mark Cathedral was never built. Within six years, the membership grew to 2,212. Although Reverend Redmond left in 1937, he left members with this mantra, in the language of the poet Sam Walter Foss: "Let me live in my house by the side of the road and be a friend of man."

From left to right are church founders John A. and Flora Washington and Henry and Nellie Bomar. Other founders were Mr. and Mrs. Richard E. Moore, Richard Jones, and George T. Jackson. In 1895, Rev. George E. Curry was sent from the Lexington Conference to Chicago and formed a permanent African American Methodist presence in Chicago. He met at the home of the Washingtons; also present were the other founders. Several other loyal Methodists were ready to go forward: Martha Trausau; Mary Thomas, and Lucille Preston. This was the beginning of what is now St. Mark United Methodist Church.

In 1895, the church moved from Thirty-Third and State Streets to 4645 South State Street, a building vacated by a white congregation because of fire. Here the St. Mark membership remained until 1897, when the congregation that had vacated the church resumed worship in their old building.

Pictured is the Fiftieth Street building used before the new church auditorium was built. In 1909, during the pastorate of Rev. W.C. Stovall, St. Mark purchased and began operating the property on Wabash Avenue at Fiftieth Street for Sunday school. St. Mark later built the main auditorium that would become known nationwide. In 1910, with the return of Rev. J.W. Robinson and the financial success of the "Gold Bond" project, the building of the new adjoining auditorium to the Sunday school was possible.

Pictured is J.A. Washington, the founder of St. Mark's choir. In 1895, St. Mark's choir had a small beginning of about seven members under the leadership of Washington, one of the founders. Nellie Bomar was organist. Washington and Bomar served faithfully for close to 25 years. During this time, membership grew to 45. Washington was followed by Walter E. Gossette as choir director.

Alma Porter Childress was born on November 20, 1894, in Durant, Mississippi. After leaving a teaching career in Mississippi, she moved to Chicago and in 1925 joined St. Mark. This devoted member was one of the pillars of the church who inspired various benevolence efforts. She was known for her care of the sick and shut-in as well as the incarcerated. She was a member of the Church Federation of Greater Chicago, a teacher in the junior department of the Sunday school, and later became Sunday school superintendent. She was honored for 67 years of dedicated service to the church. Alma Porter Childress was 97 when she died.

In Loving Memory Of

Alma Childress

WEDNESDAY, JANUARY 22, 1992

Wake – 7:00 P.M. Funeral – 7:30 P.M.

ST. MARK METHODIST CHURCH

8441 S. St Lawrence

Chicago, Illinois

*Reverend Charles Wesley Jordan – Officiating*

Rube Foster was the most prolific player in black baseball history. His most powerful years were from 1911 to 1926. He was the manager/owner of the Chicago American Giants of the Negro Baseball League. He is memorialized with a US postage stamp in his honor. This brilliant athlete died December 9, 1930. His funeral was held at St. Mark and he is buried in Lincoln cemetery.

Melinda Caroline McKissack and Robert Elias were a married couple who moved to Chicago from Nashville around 1912. They left a powerful legacy with St. Mark that lives with the congregation to this day.

# *Two*

# Building the Future

## Upon this Rock I Will Build My Church, 1935–1958

*The Scriptures teach us that God is well pleased with those who build temples to His name. We have heard how He filled the temple of Solomon with His glory, and how in the second temple He manifested Himself still more gloriously. And the gospel approves and commends the centurion who built a synagogue for the people. Let us not doubt that He will also favorably approve our purpose of dedicating this place in a solemn manner and in prayer for His further blessing upon all who have been engaged and upon all who shall hereafter worship His name in this place.*

—John W. Robinson, Pastor, 1915

In 1939, the tenure of Rev. Samuel Sweeney began at St. Mark. While this was a short sojourn for Reverend Sweeney, significant events took place during his pastorate at St. Mark. In 1938, there was the establishment of a business and professional organization by three members of the church—Zedrick T. Braden Sr., Charles Crook, and Ernest Wilkins. The Boy Scouts reorganized as Troop 534 in 1938, with Leonard O. Lee as scoutmaster. Also in 1938, the Girl Scouts were organized at St. Mark, with Dorothy Porter Welles as the troop leader.

In 1939, a historic event took place: the uniting of the church conference in Kansas City, where the Methodist Episcopal Church North, the Methodist Episcopal Church South, and the Methodist Protestant Church were consolidated into one body—the Methodist Church.

That same year, Reverend Sweeney was transferred by the conference to St. Mark Church in New York. The Sweeney Circle was formed in his honor. In 1940, Rev. Matthew W. Clair Jr. began his 12-year tenure as senior pastor of St. Mark. Many organizations emerged or expanded during his tenure. The *Voice*, a St. Mark newspaper, was first published in 1941, and in 1942 the Methodist Brotherhood became the Methodist Men. They initiated the Sunday Breakfast Fellowship. The church school grew so quickly that by 1944, two church schools, a morning church school as well as an afternoon church school, operated at full capacity.

During the week of February 20–27, 1944, the church celebrated its 50th anniversary and 50 years of service. An excerpt from the forward to the souvenir book for the occasion reads:

> We are marking a half century of Christian service. Fifty years ago when Chicago was still young, a small but determined group became interested in the beginning of Methodism, among the people of our group. Vital events have occurred since that time. Chicago has matured and become the cultural center of the middle-west, and one of the leading cities of the world. The small group which started in the home of Mr. and Mrs. J.A. Washington, has become one of the leading churches in Chicago. It ranks among the outstanding churches in Methodism.
>
> We pause to pay tribute to the past, to evaluate the present and to accept the challenges of the future.

In 1945, Rev. Samuel Wright was appointed associate pastor, and in 1947 there was the arrival of Rev. Maceo D. Pembroke as student assistant youth minister. Under Reverend Clair's pastorate, a St. Mark's baseball team was formed, as well as the St. Mark Church orchestra.

In 1952, Rev. M.W. Clair Jr. left St. Mark to become district superintendent of the Columbus District of the Lexington Conference. That year as well, Rev. Damon P. Young continued the legacy of senior pastors at St. Mark. There were to be dramatic changes in St. Mark during the tenure of Reverend Young. In 1955, St. Mark's Credit Union was incorporated, the birthday calendar was initiated, and the sunrise service was established for Easter Sunday. The growing congregation and leadership decided to expand the church facility. In 1959, after 40 years at Fiftieth Street and Wabash Avenue, St. Mark purchased the Lorimer Memorial Church, formerly a white Baptist congregation, at 8441 St. Lawrence Avenue.

St. Mark built this edifice by adding to the existing building on Fiftieth Street and Wabash Avenue that was used to conduct large Sunday school classes. By April 1923, St. Mark had cleared its debt and had a membership of 2,200. It was the leading church in the Lexington Conference and considered the mother church.

Shown are mortician Charles Crook and Rev. Hezekiah Malone, who is all ears as he listens to Crook relate the experiences he had on his 49-day trip around the world. Mr. and Mrs. Crook traveled with several friends on the trip of a lifetime in 1964. He was the owner of the Crook Ambulance service, the only black 24-hour, seven-day service to those living in the Bronzeville area during that time.

Rev. Matthew W. Clair Jr. left St. Mark in 1952 after serving 12 years. He would later become a bishop, as was his father, Bishop Matthew Clair Sr., who was elected bishop in the Methodist Episcopal Church.

Here is a younger Reverend Clair Jr. in his Army uniform when he served as chaplain and later established the only USO facilities for African Americans at Great Lakes Naval Base and at Fort Sheridan Army Base during World War II.

Shown is a memorial plaque in commemoration of Bishop Matthew Clair Sr.

Bishops Matthew Wesley Clair Sr. (right) and Matthew Wesley Clair Jr. are seen together in this rare photograph.

Local preacher Dennis Leach was an avid supporter of the Willing Workers Circle of the Women's Society of Christian Service. They were just one of many mission groups operating within the circle of Methodism in the local church. The Willing Workers were organized in 1917 under Rev. J.W. Robinson and were one of the great contributing factors in the growth and development of the church. One of the things the organization is remembered for is its gift of the baptismal fount.

In 1943, member Henry Rivers became the first African American to be appointed manager of a store within the A&P grocery store chain. The store at 5039 South Prairie Avenue was just a few blocks from the church.

The Master's Queenly Reserves (MQRs) fell under the umbrella of the Women's Foreign Missionary Society and later the WSCS. The MQRs are responsible for beginning St. Mark's homecoming services for shut-ins.

Robert A. Crolley became the first African American trustee to the Methodist Publishing House in Chicago, where he became manager of the billing department. Crolley also represented the Lexington Conference at many of the general conferences of the Methodist Church.

Pictured is the trustee board of 1944. Among them are W.H. Higgins, Charles Crook, J. Ernest Wilkins, T.M. Smith, a Mr. Broxton, and Rev. Dennis Leach.

St. Mark was blessed with 1,200 members in Sunday school. In order to accommodate the size of the 1944 classes, some groups met in the morning and some in the afternoon.

Pictured together are one of the morning classes and one of the afternoon classes. Kneeling to the left is James Hunt, and to the right are Howard Adams and Leonard O. Lee. Standing to the left are superintendent W.H. Higgins, DeWitt Lusk, and Irma Lumbar, the latter two teachers. All were outstanding examples for the children to emulate.

Girl Scout Troop 1724 was organized in 1938. On the right is troop leader Dorothy Porter Wells.

Pictured are the 1944 ushers and stewards with Rev. Matthew W. Clair and Rev. John Johnson.

Preceding the United Methodist Men was the Men's Brotherhood of St. Mark. The brotherhood was mostly made up of members employed as porters, waiters, and cooks by the railroad company. This picture is important because it shows a civic organization for African American men before society allowed them membership in other groups.

Pictured are coach W.H. Higgins and the St. Mark baseball team of 1937.

J. Ernest Wilkins Sr. was extremely active within the Methodist church and was the first African American to serve on the judicial council. At St. Mark he served as its first lay leader, a trustee, and was a member of the Lexington Conference delegation at the general conference. Beyond the church, Wilkins was the assistant secretary of labor under Pres. Dwight D. Eisenhower, becoming the first African American to serve in a subcabinet position.

J. Ernest Wilkins Jr., a prominent member of St. Mark, was nurtured in the church and was the grandson of Rev. John H. Robinson. Wilkins entered the University of Chicago at the age of 13 and graduated at the age of 19 with a doctorate in mathematics. He worked on the Manhattan Project at the University of Chicago with Enrique Fermi, and in later years helped to establish the doctoral program in mathematics at Howard University in Washington, DC, the first such program in the nation at a historically black university.

Lucille Bernice Wilkins, wife of J. Ernest Wilkins Sr., was highly active in the mission work of the church. Her services took her to the Women's Division, where she served in the early 1940s. She was the daughter of Reverend Robinson.

Pictured is a newspaper article about the US Commission on Civil Rights, established in 1957 by Pres. Dwight D. Eisenhower. St. Mark was represented on the commission by J. Ernest Wilkins (second from left); to his left sits the president of Notre Dame University, Fr. Theodore Hesburgh.

CHICAGO.SUNTIMES.COM | CHICAGO SUN-TIMES | TUESDAY, APRIL 12, 2016 | 21

OPINION

# eviue U.S. Commission on Civil Rights

JESSE JACKSON

This country has made remarkable progress on civil rights over our history. We've moved from slavery to segregation to equal rights under the law. African-Americans have gained the right to vote, the right to equal employment opportunity. Open racism has become increasingly unacceptable. Gays and lesbians have progressed toward equal rights. Same-sex marriage is increasingly accepted in law and in practice.

Yet in the past years we've been presented with inescapable evidence of continuing systemic discrimination. Ferguson and many other abuses sparked the Black Lives Matter movement that exposed the systemic and too often deadly bias of our criminal justice system.

Liberals and conservatives alike have criticized mass incarceration of nonviolent offenders, disproportionately people of color.

The wealth gap between the races has increased dramatically, as African-Americans and Latinos were disproportionately targeted and victimized by the systemic fraud that led to the financial collapse.

Muslim communities have come under brutal assault from political candidates looking to scare up votes. As we've already seen in Arizona and Wisconsin, voting rights have come under the worst

The first meeting of the U.S. Civil Rights Commission, in 1958.

The U.S. Civil Rights Commission was created in 1957 under Republican President Dwight D. Eisenhower to provide a powerful, independent monitor of civil rights. Ike's committee that recommended its formation concluded: "In a democratic society, the systematic, critical review of

1990. In 2000, it released a powerful report on police practices and civil rights in America.

The commission still exists, but it has been weakened dramatically. Under Ronald Reagan, its budget was cut. Under George W. Bush, it

*The Civil Rights Commission is a shell of its*

relations, school bullying and immigration detention — have received little attention. Its staff has been cut by more than half from its 1996 level. Its authorization has expired; it exists on annual appropriations that have slowly starved

country's leaders and its people understand the challenges we faced and recommend reforms to address them.

Now we are deprived of that powerful voice. Everything seems reduced to partisan argument. Even where there is consensus, there is no authoritative, indepen-

The St. Mark Methodist Church senior choir of 1944 flanks Walter Gossett (center left), organist/choirmaster, and Reverend Clair (center right), senior pastor. The choir was organized in 1895 with only seven members under the direction of two of St. Mark's founders, John Washington and Nellie Bomar, who was also the organist. After 25 years, they were succeeded by Walter Gossette, who served for four years as organist and choirmaster. He was followed by Cleo Dickerson Holloway, with Wesley Jones as guest conductor. On July 1, 1933, Gossette returned as organist and choirmaster.

Marie McFarland was born on November 3, 1896, in Lexington, Kentucky. She served Methodism in general and St. Mark in particular. Among her many contributions, she was a delegate to the World Federation of Methodists in Oslo, Norway, and London, England, from the Central Jurisdiction, and a delegate to the Jurisdictional Conference in 1972. She was the first black woman at this level from the Rock River Conference to serve as secretary of missionary education and service. A staunch church worker and member of St. Mark since 1922, she died on September 6, 1992, at 96 years old.

The first confirmation class of the church was initiated in 1948 by assistant pastor Reverend Pembroke. There were quite a few 12-year-olds who learned not only the methodology of the church but also what it meant to profess Christianity.

Rev. George Tate served as assistant pastor and Methodist Youth Fellowship leader. He later became the first pastor of St. Luke Methodist Episcopal Church after St. Mark's move to the Chatham neighborhood.

This panoramic photograph of the St. Mark congregation was taken around 1937 in front of St. Mark Church when it was located at Fiftieth Street and Wabash Avenue. The photograph was donated to the church by Vivian Griffin.

# *Three*

# New Horizons

## For Everything There is a Season, 1959–1999

*On Sunday, July 2, 1959 at 9 a.m. members of St. Mark Church assembled in front of the old church, [50th and Wabash Ave.] from where a 400 car motorcade drove to the newly purchased structure for morning service [84th and St. Lawrence] . . . Rev. Young described the activities for the day as a program of "entry, possession, thanksgiving and praise."*

—the *Bulletin*

The year 1959 was when St. Mark Methodist Church focused its vision on new horizons. July 9, 1959, was the day of the long-expected move. The St. Mark congregation was leaving its spiritual sanctuary that it had called home for over 40 years. Now it was a new season led by Damon Young, the senior pastor. The *Bulletin*, a community newspaper, dramatically reported the move in the July 9, 1959, issue. The purchase of Lorimer Memorial Baptist Church at 8441 South St. Lawrence Avenue also marked the final year of the Lexington Conference. The last conference was held at St. Mark. The 1960 unification of the conferences led to a name change in 1968 from St. Mark Methodist Church to St. Mark United Methodist Church.

In 1960, yet another change was on the horizon: Rev. Maceo D. Pembroke was assigned as senior pastor to St. Mark. He had been the student assistant youth minister in 1947 for Rev. Matthew W. Clair Jr. Rev. Hezekiah M. Malone became the associate pastor and Rev. Gerald Forshey became St. Mark's first Caucasian associate pastor.

In 1963, the incomparable Charles G. Kendrick became the choirmaster and organist of the chancel choir. Kendrick was the maestro of maestros. He directed five choirs: the landmark chancel choir, women's chorus, men's chorus, motet singers, and the handbell choir. With his calm demeanor, Kendrick led his choirs through some amazing times such as Glory 79–80 at Chicago's storied Auditorium Theatre. Glory 79–80 was a concert in celebration of the 80th anniversary of the founding of St. Mark. After 54 years of glorious service, the maestro retired. Dr. Robert Morris, a musician and composer, briefly served as interim choir director immediately following Kendrick's retirement. Continuing the legacy of outstanding musical leadership within the department, the elegant and scholarly Robert Neal entered as the permanent replacement. In a historical gesture, the retiring impresario passed the baton to Robert Neal at the 2017 performance of Handel's *Messiah*.

St. Mark has many superb singers, but one diva was raised in St. Mark: Jonita Lattimore sang in the children's choir under the direction of Evelyn Gaston. Lattimore is a critically acclaimed opera singer who has traveled the world and speaks several languages. Despite the demand for her stellar performances, she often sings as soprano soloist in the chancel choir's presentation of the *Messiah*. This makes her truly a diva extraordinaire.

In 1967, the Women's Society of Christian Service became the United Methodist Women. In 1969, with the support of Rev. Maceo D. Premroke Sr. and under the leadership of Bettie W. Bell and Elmontie Owens, members began laying the groundwork for the gospel choir. The first rehearsal was held on July 21, 1969, with Bell as the pianist and Owens as the director. The gospel choir made its debut on Sunday, August 4, 1969, at the 9:30 a.m. service. In 1973, the spirited Rev. Francine Taylor-Thirus served as codirector. In 1990, after 21 years of service, Bettie Bell retired as the director of the choir. Enter Karen Susan Lee, who became a member of St. Mark when she was a child. Lee was mentored and received formal training from Charles G. Kendrick, minister of music at St. Mark.

In the 1990s, Karen Lee became the director. In 2002, she was joined by Prentice Smith, who served as codirector of the gospel choir. Smith joined the St. Mark Music Department on a full-time basis in 2005. The gospel choir continued to grow under the leadership of Lee and Smith, until the untimely death of Prentice Smith in the spring of 2007. Karen Lee continued to lead the gospel choir, Commissioned for Christ, and the praise team at St. Mark. On September 14, 2008, her gifted hands were silenced with her sudden death. In honor of the beloved director, the St. Mark gospel choir was named the Karen S. Lee Memorial Gospel Choir.

Aaron Cockerham and Blanche Adams Body stepped in to provide direction for the choir from October until Christmas 2008. Rev. James Bryson Jr. served as interim director from 2008 until he was permanently appointed in July 2009. With his charismatic personality, Reverend Bryson made a significant impact on the members of the gospel choir as well as the entire church family. In 2016, Reverend Bryson left the gospel choir to accept the position of lead pastor at First Church of Deliverance. In 2017, the Karen S. Lee Memorial Gospel Choir was blessed with the gifted Semaj Coleman.

In 1973, Rev. B. Herbert Martin was appointed associate pastor, and in 1977, Rev. Tallulah Fisher Williams was appointed the first female associate pastor. Reverend Williams impressed the congregation with her very spirited sermons: memorable ones include "Why We Sing the Blues" and "The Eagle and the Chicken." During the late 1970s, Pearl Day, a lay leader, reestablished the United Methodist Youth Fellowship (UMYF). In 1979, Edith Clark organized the first blood drive and later passed the torch to Juanita Dean.

In 1981, the quiet giant, Rev. Maceo D. Pembroke, died, ending an incredible era for St. Mark United Methodist Church. That same year, Rev. Harry B. Gibson Jr. was appointed senior pastor of St. Mark. Rev. Myron F. McCoy and Rev. Jacob C. Williams Jr. arrived shortly thereafter as associate ministers of St. Mark. They became a dynamic trio due to the spiritual energy they brought to the congregation. The acolytes program emerged in 1982, as did the Innovators, a young adult ministry. In 1983, St. Mark celebrated 90 years of service to the Chicago community. The dynamic trio ended with the departure of Reverend McCoy and Reverend Williams. The church was soon blessed with a bounty of three new dynamic and innovative associate pastors: Rev. Danita Anderson, Rev. Larry D. Pickens, and Rev. Keith Kelsey-Powell.

The late 1980s and 1990s saw Harry B. Gibson deliver his farewell sermon to the St. Mark congregation, as well as the passing of one of St. Mark's most devoted members, Marie F. McFarland, and the formation of the Liturgical Dance Ministry organized by Shirley Hobson in 1997, with Kristen and Kelly McCord as choreographers. With the sweet harmony of their steps, they led St. Mark into another century.

"A Century of Praise"

O God we sing to Thee a Century of Praise
We Worship you with mem'ries of our blessed days.
With grateful heart we bow as heirs to Christian gold.
Such treasures of St. Mark as unto us bestowed.
We thank you God for those who've passed along our way.
Their pioneering soul has given us this day.
Oh make us worthy Lord in Spirit and in mind,
That we may keep the St. Mark heritage divine.

—Lucius Bell

Reverend Pembroke and baptismal stewards Sadie Anderson and Betty Green Walker joyfully participate in the baptism of three-month-old Cynthia Lusk. Anderson served in this capacity for more than 50 years.

Theodore Charles Stone from the Chicago Music Association looks on as organist and choir director Walter Gossett is presented a plaque for his service over numerous years to the choir by Evelyn Gaston. Gossett has, to his credit, accompanied Marian Anderson, who recognized him at one of her concerts.

Pictured is the 1981 confirmation class with Rev. Tullulah Fisher Williams, instructor.

Halloween Fun Night was an event where adults as well as children dressed for a safe night of fun with movies, costume parades, prizes, and activities. It was sponsored by the United Methodist Women initially and later by the Sunday school.

Rev. Gerald Forshay became the first cross-racial appointment to the church; thus, St. Mark became the only church to have an integrated ministerial staff when the Lexington and Rock River Conferences merged in 1964. Forshay was a participant in the Selma, Alabama, march with Dr. Martin Luther King Jr. His wife, Florence, was a member of the chancel choir for more than 40 years, remaining at St. Mark after he was appointed elsewhere.

A yearly event looked forward to is the honor bestowed upon the men of the church by the United Methodist Men. Man of the Year is a coveted award that has been given to eight past honorees. Pictured are (seated) Othello Ellis, Robert Tucker, and Byron Dean Sr.; (standing) Prince Clayton, James McQuirter, Lucas Clarkston, and George Moultrie.

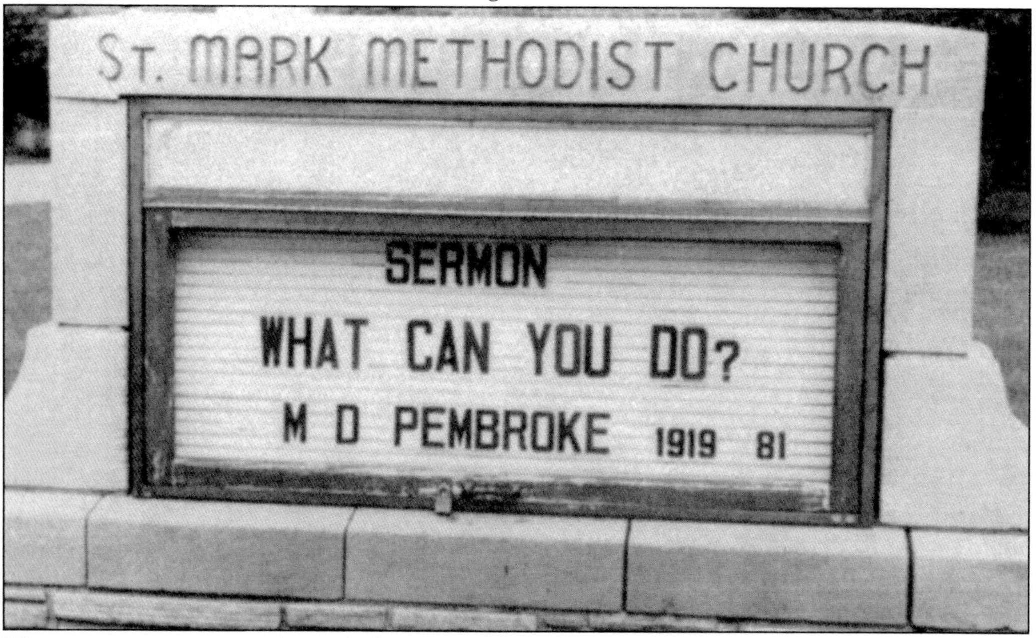


The marquee announces the end of an era with the death of Rev. Maceo D. Pembroke. He served St. Mark as senior pastor from 1961 to 1981.

Pictured is Homecoming Sunday for members who were no longer able to attend worship services on a regular basis. They were transported by bus and picked up by members in order to have as many present as possible, after which they had lunch together before returning home.

Betty W. Bell founded the gospel choir at Eighty-Fourth and St. Lawrence Streets in 1969. With the support of Rev. Maceo D. Pembroke Sr., the first rehearsal was held on July 21, 1969. Bell took the choir to many highs, winning several awards. She retired from the choir in 1990 after 21 years of glorious service.

Partners was organized by Rev. Maceo Pembroke for the sole purpose of fellowship among couples within the church. After the death of several spouses, the group chose to stay together and was renamed the Forever Partners.

The men's chorus, organized in 1964, included O.P. Gaston, Clint Ward, Walter Richards, William Bell, Arvarh Strickland, and Charles Brooks, who surround director Prince Marshall, interim director Rev. Maceo Pembroke, and Rev. Malone.

St. Mark men's chorus is but one of the many choirs formed to enhance the worship services of the church. In addition to lifting their melodic voices on Sundays, they sang at special programs honoring men of the church. Pictured are members in 1968.

Dr. T. Manuel Smith was considered a bedrock for St. Mark in terms of his benevolent giving. His love for God and St. Mark Church was evident in many ways. His many monetary gifts enabled the mission of the church to be carried out to a greater degree. Dr. Smith was a cardiologist, and his mild-mannered, caring personality endeared him to patients and church members alike.

Pictured is a souvenir book from the 90th anniversary of St. Mark.

This is a c. 1980 St. Mark basketball team, with coach Wiley Jackson seated at right.

St. Mark United Methodist Church

presents

SEVEN CHOIR CONCERT

GLORY
'79

*"Praising God in Song"*

SUNDAY, JUNE 17, 1979
AUDITORIUM THEATRE

Rev. Maceo D. Pembroke, Pastor
Rev. Tullulah F. Williams, Associate
Rev. Martin G. McCain, Associate

Music Department
Charles Kendrick, Director
Betty Bell, Evelyn Gaston, Fracine Thirus

Glory '79—one just had to be there to experience the heartwarming pride of this St. Mark presentation at the famed Auditorium Theatre. The vinyl records still bring joy to listeners. It was seven choirs, a full house, and an appreciative swelling of applause.

Pictured are Rev. Dennis Hutson, former church secretary, and his wife, Patricia. He is one of 30 persons recruited into the ministry by Rev. Maceo Pembroke. Reverend Hutson served 20 years as a chaplain in the US Air Force and was responsible for assigning Protestant chaplains all over the world.

Rev. Harry Gibson is with Harold Washington as the congressman from Illinois addresses voters at a St. Mark campaign stop. Washington became the first African American elected as mayor of the city of Chicago, serving from 1983 to 1987.

Centenarian Nell Hunter, a member of the chancel choir, passed away the age of 103; at the age of 100, she had celebrated her birthday by giving a vocal concert at St. Mark.

All eight of the St. Mark choirs sang at Praising God in Song, Glory 79–80, a concert performed at the Chicago Auditorium Theatre on June 22, 1980.

Dr. J. Herbert Touchstone was the first recipient of St. Mark's Man of the Year award. This recognition is given yearly for outstanding service. Dr. Touchstone traveled as a member of the board of laity, promoting Methodist men's groups nationwide. He taught at the historically black college Philander Smith for more than 30 years.

The church sign proudly announces Vice Pres. Walter Mondale's campaign stop at St. Mark. He served as vice president to Jimmy Carter (1977–1981), and both sought reelection to a second term. Shown below is Mondale's address to the congregation at the end of the worship service.

Joyce Favors served as director of Christian education for more than 20 years. She is responsible for initiating the Disciple Bible Studies program at St. Mark.

Pictured is the St. Mark children's choir during the late 1980s, with Evelyn Gaston, a director who was able to work wonders with voices that were changing as she did three-part selections.

Chicago Public Schools, the second-largest educational system in the country at the time, came under the supervision of Ruth Love as superintendent of schools. While here, she became a member of St. Mark—to the delight of some of the many educator-members of the church.

In 1984, Dennis Leach, a longtime member of St. Mark, celebrates his 100th birthday with Rev. Harry B. Gibson Jr. and Hazel Marion, the founder of Partners in Retirement. Leach was one of the first to join Partners in Retirement.

A photography trailblazer who went from the old methods of the Van DerZee era to digital cameras, Willie Griffin was a man for all seasons. He established the St. Mark Camera Club to record all events and activities for perpetuity. To his credit, the club participates in photography competitions and hosts art exhibits and an annual awards luncheon. Club members strive to stay abreast of new technology and techniques to promote a better experience with the camera.

Pictured is the Chicago Black Methodists for Church Renewal staff and several local members. From left to right are Tracy Broadnax, Rev. Sylvester Brinson III, Marilyn McGee Butler, executive director Rev. William "Bill" Carter, Ruth Thompson, Rev. Dwight Stewart, and Nodie Sampson. Not pictured is Marc Dean, staff assistant to the director in the 1970s.

The Moultrie brothers, George and John, were instrumental in bringing to the church a credit union. It is still thriving as an aid for savings and financial help to members today.

Among those pictured here are Reverend Pembroke and Dr. John Hope Franklin, the celebrated African American historian.

The 100th anniversary of the church featured Heritage Sunday, with members dressed in 1893 attire. Mattie Houston and Percival Harmon look as if they are on their way to church at founders John and Flora Washington's home.

Linda White, former national president of the Alpha Kappa Alpha sorority and lifetime member of St. Mark, was the featured speaker one year for the UMW's Women's Day.

Delta Sigma Theta members of St. Mark are shown flanking Dr. Johnetta Cole (center), former president of Spellman and Bennett Colleges. Bennett is a United Methodist college and one of the historically black colleges and universities (HBCUs).

George Eugene is the only St. Mark Boy Scout to have traveled across the ocean with troops from the Chicago area. He represented St. Mark at the jamboree in Brisbane, Australia, which lasted for 10 days in 1988.

Micah Morgan, son of Laura and Dr. Herman Morgan, and Kevin Hale, son of Betty and Toussaint Hale, highlight the pride St. Mark takes in young men who went through Sunday school, entered the United States Naval Academy, and graduated in the class of 1983 as midshipmen first class. They have since retired with honors after serving 20 years as successful senior officers.

Two St. Mark members who reigned over the educational pursuits of young people seeking higher educational achievements were Dr. Benjamin Alexander, president of Chicago State University, and Dr. Ronald Temple, chancellor for the City Colleges of Chicago, the second-largest city college system in the country. Dr. Temple also holds the rank of Eagle Scout in St. Mark Scouting.

St. Mark members were avid supporters of Carol Mosley Braun during her campaign for US senator. She became the first African American woman to be elected senator (1993–1999) and only the second African American (after Edward Brooke III of Massachusetts in 1966) elected to the Senate since Reconstruction. Braun had earlier served in the Illinois House and later served as US ambassador to New Zealand and Samoa.

The St. Mark Communication Committee held the responsibility for early issues of the *Voice* and *United Methodist Reporter* articles. Pictured are (standing) James Hunt, Don Gibson, Wiley Jackson, and Charles Brooks; (seated) Delores Brothers, Loretta Rias, Stanley Brothers, Anna MacLin, and Mattie West.

The 100th Anniversary Committee, chaired by Sandra Givens (seated, far left), gave St. Mark a celebratory event monthly, in addition to the publication of the *St. Mark Cookbook* organized by Byron and Juanita Dean.

St. Mark women were honored at a United Methodist Women reception for 50 years of participation in the organization. From left to right are Bettie Lusk, Vivian Griffin, Juanita Dean, and Naomi Hall.

Roland Burris, a resident of the Chatham community, is seen on one of his many visits to St. Mark to address the importance of participating in the political system by voting. He has held sundry political titles, the last of which was US senator.

Pictured are Charles and Virginia Tatum with senior pastor Rev. Myron McCoy. Tatum was the innovator for the creation of St. Mark Manor, the church's senior housing. He also served as a trustee for Garrett Evangelical Theological Seminary (GETS).

Bishop Tracy Smith Malone (center), currently over the East Ohio Conference of the United Methodist Church, served her pre-graduate divinity years as a seminarian for St. Mark. She served several Northern Illinois Conference (NIC) churches before her election to the episcopacy in 2017. Pictured are Brenda Hambright, Rev. Barbara Morgan, UMW president Delores Cooper, and Pamelle Readus.

Helen Fannings Ammons represented the Methodist Church on many general boards and agencies. As a staff member of GETS, she gave counsel and guidance and befriended prospective clergy. She is the spouse of the late Bishop Edsel Ammons.

Some St. Markers and friends set sail on a Norwegian Cruise Lines vessel as a fundraiser for the Phase II Building Fund Project. Like Cinderella, they are pictured making their special staircase entrance to the Captain's Ball, after which they became known as "those sophisticated St. Markers."

Featured St. Mark revival speaker Rev. Dr. Zann Holmes is surrounded by the ministerial team of St. Mark. Reverend Holmes was featured as commentator in the very first Disciple Bible Study program. From left to right are Revs. Amos Oladipo, Barbara Morgan, Dr. Henry Young (St. Mark interim pastor and professor at Garrett Evangelical Seminary), Zann Holmes, Tracy Smith Malone, and Michelle Taylor Sanders.

St. Mark hosted and housed teenage boys and young men who fled the horrors confronting the Sudanese people. A meet and greet was held in their honor.

Pictured are St. Mark participants in the historic Million Man March on Washington in 1998.

Emma Thomas, an esteemed Girl Scout troop leader, was one among an endless line of splendid leadership that existed as far back as the 1940s. During her tenure, St. Mark was recognized as having among the highest Girl Scout cookie sales in the city of Chicago.

Shirley Hobson, founder, was the dynamic creative force behind the liturgical dance ministry at St. Mark.

Pictured is one of the early liturgical dance troupes with choreographer Kimberly Leonard (standing at far left) and the dance ministry's originator, Shirley Hobson, standing at far right.

The gleeful liturgical dance troupe is about to get into formation and execute one of its graceful dance routines.

Miracle Sunday took place on Sunday, June 2, 1991. The plaque commemorates this date because it was the time when St. Mark donated enough gifts to fund a second elevator for St. Mark Manor. The manor was erected as a residence for seniors.

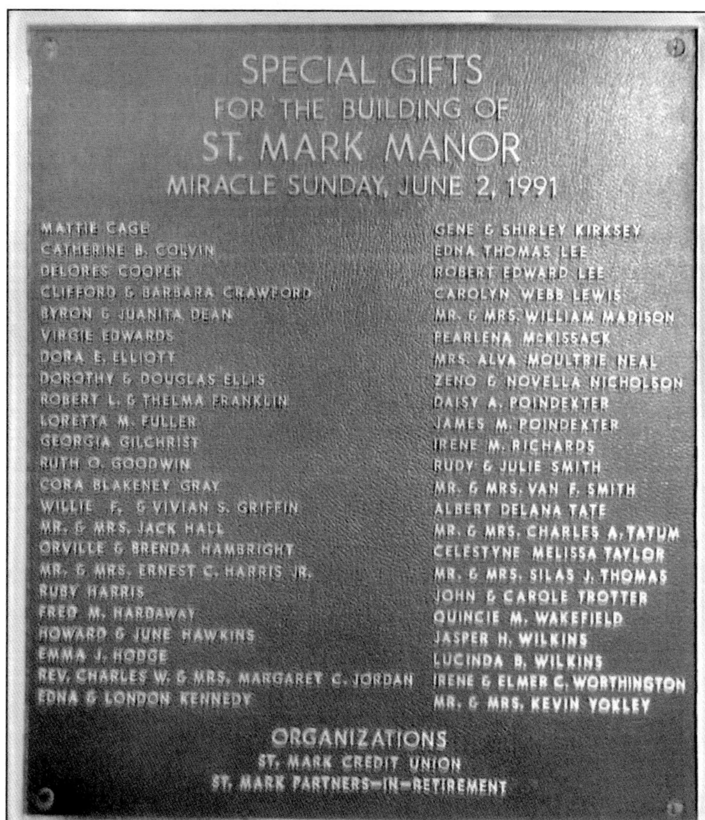

# *Four*

# Looking to the Future:

## Your Old Shall Dream Dreams; Your Young Shall See Visions, 2000–2018

*As we embark on celebrating 125 years of St. Mark United Methodist Church, I am reflective of the nurturing, love, religious training and support I received as a member of St. Mark UMC. I do believe that my membership at St. Mark has stamped a significant impression on my outlook with the love of God, family and career, as I continue to navigate and chart my life's journey.*

—Brandon G. Draper

The year 2000 marked a new year and a new century. Would St. Mark be ready for the challenges that lay ahead? Looking toward their ancestors, and with faith as tiny as a mustard seed, members of the congregation forged ahead.

In 2003, Phase II of the church expansion project was in full gear, and Rev. Myron F. McCoy accepted a position as president of St. Paul School of Theology in Kansas City, Missouri. Rev. Henry Young served as interim pastor from 2003 through 2004, a period of challenge and change.

In March 2004, Rev. Dr. Jon E. McCoy was installed as senior pastor by district superintendent Rev. Donald Guest. St. Mark adopted Reverend McCoy's message of *Press Toward the Mark* as the new church motto, thereby retiring *Pass it On*. In 2004, the church received Rev. Ricky Georgetown as an associate pastor, followed by Rev. Minnie Davis. The Martial Arts ministry was organized in 2005 as well as the Garden Club ministry. In 2007, the Home Bible Study ministry and the Prison ministry were established. The renovation of the balcony took place in 2007 and the renovation of the transept was completed in 2010.

In 2013, the dynamic pastoral staff was introduced to the congregation: Rev. Francine Taylor-Thirus, associate pastor Rev. Adonna Reid, assistant pastor Minister Michelle Watkins, and seminarian Rev. William Andrews. In 2010, St. Markers protested the transfer of Reverend McCoy, and in 2011, McCoy received special recognition at a *Chicago Defender* event, "Pastor's Salute."

In 2012, Reverend McCoy convened a committee to launch the celebration of St. Mark's 120th anniversary. The event was a service with a historical exhibition celebrating St. Mark's history and legacy. A pictorial church history book was produced, *St. Mark United Methodist Church, Celebrating 120 Years: A Pictorial Journey 1893–2013*, which yielded substantial revenue.

There came an announcement from the NIC that Rev. Dr. Jon McCoy would be taking his spiritual leadership to Hinsdale United Methodist Church in Hinsdale, Illinois, as of July 2013. Rev. P. Devon Brown became St. Mark's new senior pastor.

Reverend Brown was no stranger to the St. Mark family, as he had served as associate pastor from 1992 to 1994. Brown previously served as senior pastor at Faith United Methodist Church. On Sunday, July 7, 2013, Reverend Brown gave his first sermon as senior pastor, "Love Alive I: A Friend With Benefits." His message, passionately presented, was very well received. By September 2013, the pastoral staff had changed again. Rev. Adonna Reid departed for another church. The church welcomed associate pastor Barbara Morgan and ministry candidate Luther Mason. Under

Reverend Brown, the Sunday morning worship times were changed to 8:00 and 10:00. In 2016, Reverend Morgan left, and St. Mark welcomed Rev. Dwight Stewart as the new associate pastor, along with his wife.

In 2016, Reverend Brown asked Daniel Parker, history chair, to chair the committee for St. Mark's 125th Anniversary. Parker called upon Violette Brooks, a former librarian, and together they mapped out a plan. The committee was convened, with many St. Markers willing to participate. The entire church and community rejoiced in its 125 anniversary.

Much of the focus of Reverend Brown's vision has been on youth. St. Mark has always had the young as part of its vision. Two of the church's young people, Brandon G. Draper and Jocelyn Moore, shared their experiences growing up in St. Mark:

> Some of my earliest memories are of family, friends, and St. Mark UMC. As a child, I attended Sunday school and participated in the Easter and Christmas plays, as well as other traditional church events. These church events played a significant role in developing my religious and personal character. I participated in the children's choir, was an acolyte, and participated in the UMYF and confirmation class. During this time, I joined BSA Troop 534 Hey, achieving the rank of Eagle Scout. The summer before I entered college, I attended an international missionary camp in New Hampshire.
>
> When I attended North Carolina Central University, I received much support and nurturing from the Higher Education Committee, always reminding me of my religious training and support from my church. The popcorn, fudge, care packages, and Walmart cards always came in handy, but more than that, I knew that my church cared about me as I was striving to complete college. My internship after my junior year was also through the church. I spent the entire summer interning with the General Board of Church and Society of the UMC, which at the time was the only religious nonprofit that lobbied on Capitol Hill. I was able to intern with the NAACP Washington Bureau in the District of Columbia. This opportunity gave me the chance to make lifelong connections, which I still use to this very day. It was truly a life-changing experience.
>
> —Brandon Draper

> I was raised by my mother, father, and St. Mark United Methodist Church. Outside of my house, my church was the next most visited building of my childhood. Driving down St. Lawrence and seeing the church on the right brings me a sense of peace.
>
> My St. Mark beginnings started with my grandmother Gussie Johnson, who I never got to meet. I'm sure she never guessed the impact her decision to join the church back in the 40s or 50s would make on her family. Did she know her daughter and granddaughter would both be married in the church, or three of her grandsons would become Eagle Scouts there? Did she know her oldest daughter would be one of the long serving members and dedicate her life to the church and women's groups? Did she picture her youngest daughter working with the youth of the church, singing in the Gospel choir and devoting her life to the church just like her big sister Charlie Mae? I'm sure she didn't see any of these things, but she did see a great church with a lot of potential that she felt comfortable in. I am so glad she did, because her decision changed my life forever.
>
> My 17 years at St. Mark truly laid the groundwork of the physician and business owner I am today. My mother and aunt kept their mother's dream alive, by raising their families in the church. My mom was able to see what the church did for her family and her sister's family. She wanted her children to reap the same benefits of a loving and encouraging church. She wanted to see us speaking in church, becoming involved in something outside of school, where we still were able to learn.
>
> —Jocelyn (Moore) Slaughter

Pictured is Jeremy Rembert leading children's time.

This photograph of St. Mark congregation members includes representatives from all four periods of the church's history. The 125th anniversary committee divided the congregation into four periods of church history, based on when a member joined St. Mark. Trailblazers (1893–1959) are members who began and carried the legacy of St. Mark from its early roots. Connectors (1959–1980) are members who acted as change agents connecting the old Wabash Avenue church and its traditions to the new church, through the Civil Rights Era, and into more recent times. Innovators (1980–2000) are members who creatively prepared St. Mark for the new millennium and the challenges of new technology. New Generation (2000–present) are members who incorporate social media, the latest technology, and creative thinking in leading the St. Mark congregation into the "brave new world" while spreading the same hopeful message.

Pictured are New Generation members.

Shown is the 2012 Sunday school class. St. Mark is committed to youth involvement in the life of the church at all age levels and helps to hone spiritual and life skills.

Pictured here is the St. Mark Golf Club of 2003. For many years, the club traveled to Memphis, Tennessee, for its annual outing and tournament. It was hosted there by Tim and Helen Jones, former members of both St. Mark and the golf club.

Pictured are Rev. Minnie Davis and Rev. Jon McCoy.

These Volunteers in Mission were celebrated during one worship service. From left to right are Rev. Minnie Davis, Ralph Cross, Laura Morgan, Mel Ervin, Patricia Phillips, Rev. Karli Pigeon, Deborah Lindsey, Patricia Evans, and Wiley Jackson.

These are the St. Mark clergy and invited guest speakers at the Good Friday service in 2013. From left to right are (first row) Rev. Michelle Watkins-Branch; Rev. Francine Taylor-Thirus; Rev. Sally Dyck, NIC, UMC; associate pastor Barbara Morgan; and Rev. William Andrews, seminarian, with ministry candidate Luther Mason standing behind him; (second row) Bishop Tracy Malone; Rev. Dr. Jon McCoy, senior pastor, SMUMC; and other unidentified bishops and speakers.

Pictured are Dorothy Brown (seated, center), Cook County clerk of the circuit court, and Rev. Michelle Taylor (seated, left of Brown) with Lydia Circle members at the annual prayer breakfast sponsored by the UMW.

Rev. Dr. Jacques Conway, district superintendent of the Chicago Southern District (NIC), addresses the congregation.

Pictured is the annual Charge conference conducted by Rev. Dr. Jacques A. Conway, district superintendent of the Chicago Southern District (NIC). Seated are Rev. P. Devon Brown and Gerald Jordan.

Pictured are Rev. James Bryson, director of the Karen S. Lee Memorial Gospel Choir, Charles Redmond, singing, and Ralph Cross, background.

The St. Mark handbell choir surrounds its director, Mr. Kendricks, as it prepares a serenade of "Carol of the Bells." This is one of eight choirs at St. Mark.

Members of the Flora Washington subgroup don beautiful hats for the 2018 Women's Day services.

St. Mark's own Rev. Michelle Watkins-Branch was guest speaker at the 2018 Women's Day service. Reverend Watkins-Branch was the associate pastor under Rev. P. Devon Brown.

The United Methodist Women stand as Loretta Rias, chair, presents members with flowers. From left to right are Penny Tobias, Dorris McGill, Wilma Reynolds, Delores Cooper, Loretta Rias, and Felicia Gaines.

Here is the 2018 St. Mark's Women's Day choir singing and praising in all of its glory.

One can almost hear the angelic voices of the nursery and prekindergarten children as they proclaim their joy in song. Parents and teachers offer assurance.

Shown here is the children's choir with director Matthew Rose and his wife, Jennifer. He is the great-grandson of Rev. Matthew Clair Sr. and grandson of Bishop Matthew Clair Jr.

The Sounds of Judah, under the direction of Tracy Malloy, are an intricate part of the worship service at St. Mark. When they sing, the sounds of their majestic voices echo throughout the sanctuary.

Pictured are the Liturgical Dancers at the 125th anniversary kick-off worship service.

Shown here are members of the Liturgical Dance Ministry.

The Liturgical Dance Ministry was organized in 1997 by Shirley Hobson. Choreographers Kristin and Kelly McCord based the rhythmic movements of the dances on Scripture references or from experiences from the tree of life.

Participants in the Martial Arts Ministry, under the direction of Master Maceo Pembroke Jr., proudly show off their awards and trophies. St. Mark offers a range of youth-oriented activities.

Pictured are Vacation Bible School participants on July 14, 1971.

Pictured are members of Boy Scout Troop 534 "Hey!" They are following their motto to "Be Prepared" as they get set for a Scouting excursion.

Boy Scout Troop 534 "Hey!" is pictured during a service project (above), as well as participating in 2018 Boy Scout Sunday (below).

These young ladies are cherishing their bouquets after receiving the coveted Girl Scout Gold Award. They are flanked by their leaders, Lois Moreland Dean, left, and Virginia Reynolds. The Gold Award is one of the highest achievements a Girl Scou can receive—and the smiles on the faces of the parents and girls prove it.

The Girl Scouts of St. Mark set a record for cookie sales. St. Mark has three troops. The Brownies are No. 20346, the Cadettes are No. 20305, and the Seniors are No. 21260. Here, the Girl Scouts proudly pose with some of their cookies.

The Higher Education Ministry sponsored a luncheon to honor recent graduates for their scholastic achievements.

Confirmands are front and center after completing a challenging course of religious study. They are welcomed by Rev. P. Devon Brown, and on the right is Rev. Felix Johnson, seminarian.

Young new Christians are all smiles as they begin their faith walk. Standing by their sides are Reverend Brown on the left and Reverend Stewart at right.

St. Mark celebrates the acolytes, young people who play active roles in the opening and closing of worship services. On the left are Reverend Brown and Marcia McDonald; Kristin Andrews is on the right.

With great pleasure, this Sunday school class stands proudly with their devoted teachers.

Pictured are the St. Mark acolytes and their leaders: Kristin Andrews, left, and Marcia McDonald.

A group that included many trailblazing members who attended the church at the Fiftieth Street location gather there to begin the caravan. St. Mark was at Wabash Avenue and Fiftieth Street from 1909 to 1959.

A reenactment of the historic pilgrimage to the new church took place on August 18, 2018. With a police escort, a caravan of vehicles left from the old church building at Fiftieth Street and Wabash Avenue to the new location at Eighty-Fourth Street and St. Lawrence Avenue, announcing to the community St. Mark's 125th anniversary.

Sharon Brown is addressing the congregation at the 125th anniversary kick-off celebration. She was instrumental in creatively organizing the events arm of the 125th Anniversary Committee. To the right is Jamille Hall.

Delighted 125th Anniversary Committee members present Rev. P. Devon Brown, senior pastor (right), with a check for $12,180 for the church mortgage fund. From left to right,are Doris McGill, Regeta Slaughter, committee chairman Daniel Parker, and event committee chairwoman Sharon Brown; seated behind them is seminarian Rev. William Andrews.

Dr. Jocelyn (Moore) Slaughter, on growing up in St. Mark, states, "Every year that St. Mark actively had youth participate in the services and other special events, it helped to mold me into the confident speaker I am today. These experiences have stayed with me, and made me into a business owner. Many people ask me, 'How are you able to own a medical practice and run it at 34 years old?' 'How did you become so organized and have all of these leadership skills?' I truly believe the majority came from the core that St. Mark built in me during my childhood."

Brandon G. Draper, a college and career coach, says: "When I became a college and career coach, my goals were to inspire youth and inform them that college is possible! When I attended North Carolina Central University, I received much support and nurturing from the Higher Education Committee, always reminding me of my religious training and support from my church."

The 2018 dedicated staff of St. Mark United Methodist Church is pictured here. From left to right are senior pastor Rev P. Devon Brown; seminarian Rev. William Andrews; Rev. Atty. Francine Taylor-Thirus, retired UMC pastor; and associate pastor Rev. Dwight Stewart.

Rev. P. Devon Brown is flanked by the congregation before the service celebrating St. Mark's 125th anniversary on Sunday, September 30, 2018. A believing community gathers here to worship, and scatters to serve.

# Bibliography

Lee, Lynne. *St. Mark United Methodist Church, Celebrating 120 Years: A Pictorial Journey 1893–2013.* Chicago, IL: Clydesign.com, 2013.

_____. Pictorial church history (unpublished).

Wesleyan Service Guild. *Saint Mark's Blue Book.* Chicago, IL: St. Mark Methodist Episcopal Church, 1933.

Wilkins, Carolyn Marie. *Damn Near White: An African American Family's Rise from Slavery to Bittersweet Success.* Columbia, MO: University of Missouri Press, 2010.